AND THEY CALLED IT HORIZON

AND THEY CALLED IT HORIZON

SANTA FE POEMS *by* VALERIE MARTÍNEZ
Santa Fe Poet Laureate 2008–2010
DRAWINGS *by* LINDA SWANSON

SANTA FE

© 2010 by Valerie Martínez.
Drawings © 2010 by Linda Swanson.
All Rights Reserved.

No part of this book may be reproduced in any form or by any electronic or mechanical means including information storage and retrieval systems without permission in writing from the publisher, except by a reviewer who may quote brief passages in a review.

Sunstone books may be purchased for educational, business, or sales promotional use. For information please write: Special Markets Department, Sunstone Press, P.O. Box 2321, Santa Fe, New Mexico 87504-2321.

Book design › Vicki Ahl
Body typeface › Adobe Garamond Pro and Dauphin
Printed on acid free paper

Library of Congress Cataloging-in-Publication Data

Martínez, Valerie, 1961-
  And they called it horizon : Santa Fe poems / by Valerie Martínez ; drawings by Linda Swanson.
      p. cm.
  ISBN 978-0-86534-790-8 (softcover : alk. paper)
 1. Santa Fe (N.M.)--Poetry. I. Title.
 PS3563.A73345A85 2010
 811'.54--dc22
                                    2010042434

WWW.SUNSTONEPRESS.COM
SUNSTONE PRESS / POST OFFICE BOX 2321 / SANTA FE, NM 87504-2321 /USA
(505) 988-4418 / ORDERS ONLY (800) 243-5644 / FAX (505) 988-1025

Acknowledgments

Grateful acknowledgment is made to the following publications where these poems, in these or earlier versions, have appeared: "Blue Winding, Blue Way," *Return of the River: Writers, Scholars and Citizens Speak on Behalf of the Santa Fe River;* "Days Like These," *Poems—Dreams for the Railyard Park;* "El Mundo a Mundo," *Metamorfosis: Voces femininas, palabras español;* "On the Road to Mictlán," *Crossings: Origins and Celebrations of Día de Muertos;* sections of "New Mexico Fragments," "Childhood," and "Trying to Understand," *World to World,* University of Arizona Press, 2004.

Many thanks to the following for their advice, expertise, love and encouragement: Carolyn Kastner, David Coss, Teresa Dovalpage, Roberts French, David Grey, Tom Leech, Tom Maguire, Sabrina Pratt and the staff of the Santa Fe Arts Commission, Estevan Rael-Gálvez, Shelle Sánchez, Molly Sturges and everyone at Littleglobe, James Clois Smith, Jr., and the staff of Sunstone Press, our families, the citizens of Santa Fe and—especially—Paul, Ed, and Georgia.

Contents

Part One / 11

Blue Winding, Blue Way / 15
Santa Fe Sestina / 16
Sestina de Santa Fe / 18
Clouds / 20
Days Like This / 23
New Mexico Fragments / 29
Follow Me / 35
Hush / 36

Part Two / 39

And They Called it Horizon. / 41

Part Three / 55

Childhood / 57
Letters to Wherever You Are / 61
Art and Tennis Shoes / 65
Mid-High, 1976 / 69
I Won't Pretend / 73
History, Apology / 74
She Has Come To Us / 76

Part Four / 79

Easter Pilgrims / 81
El mundo al mundo / 85
On the Road to Mictlán / 86
Trying to Understand / 88
Street Secrets / 89
Thistle Forest / 91
River Ode / 95
Home / 103

About the Author and the Artist / 109
Notes and Translations / 111

Drawings by Linda Swanson

Swimsuits / 6
Shoulders / 13
Hiking / 21
Sunglasses / 27
Offering Snow / 33
Zozobra / 37
Father Love / 53
Braiding / 59
Burro / 63
Goofing / 67
Backbend / 71
Asleep / 77
Turn / 83
Water / 93
Family / 101
Grandma / 107

for all Santa Feans
and for the city we love

Part One

Blue Winding, Blue Way

I tell you, City, City, City, a story you told me—brown eyes, green eyes, black—in the days of snow drifts, mini-skirts, nothing beyond Richards Ave. The center of earth was a patch of land, our house, a back yard, the arroyo humming over the reddish concrete wall, and one immortal turtle. The neighbor's immense ham radio antenna and Mr. Chang hunched to static and metal under the morning buzz of Osage Ave. We went to school in sedans, in dented station wagons, and on weekends workmen showed up to build vigas for the new den that swelled our home—so many children—Alfonso saying, *mi linda, get me that bucket* and *¿donde está tu mama?* Me saying, *at the grocery store, buying tubs of ice cream, you know, those big ones? Get me, ice cream, you know* took to the air over the rooftops spilling toward Frenchy's Field. We weren't supposed to play there—*he'll shoot, you know*—and I imagined the old man hunched somewhere near the water, listening. In those days the Santa Fe River ran and sang. *It's true?* you ask, staring at the empty bed, dust rising at the dead end of Avenida Cristobal Colón. *There was water?* Now, we dream of blue winding, blue way along West Alameda—barbershop, coop, health clinic. The clog and cough of St. Francis Drive. Back then there were cars and wanderers and children just like now—towheads, dark braids, dirty cuffs—rolled up with all of us on the days of markets and parades along San Francisco and Palace Ave. *Hmmm* went the setting sun and you really could get fry bread for a quarter after walking down Washington Street from Fort Marcy after Zozobra burned. Now I drive downtown where the acequia crosses Closson and Maynard, stutters along Water Street, and sings the parallels of East Alameda and Canyon Road. Like a whisper, it lays itself down between Camino del Monte Sol and Camino Cabra, two streets with the river in-between—one with her skirt trailing southwest to the Paseo Real, the other reaching her fingernail moons to the foothills. And the river itself, dream of p'oe tsawa, flushed from the red burn of the Sangres, running headlong downhill into this city of ours, then and now, with her canciónes encantadas, with her blue, with her brown mouth open.

Santa Fe Sestina

Late autumn blows leaves into women's hair. On the plaza,
Lydia feeds the pigeons—iridescent feathers gone blue
in the tangerine sun. It is afternoon and adobe,
crush of pueblo-style hotel rooms against a sky
that holds them steady. Her skirt is wound in ribbons,
gathered in ruffles, wind-flipped velvet, black and silver.

Merrymakers tumble from the doors of La Fonda, blue
windbreakers and cowboy hats. Spun from adobe,
they rush by Lydia like a tornado. A glance at the sky
stuns them, for a moment, then they're a ribbon
of raucous laughter. Sunlight descends in silver,
travels the metal rain gutters, trimming the plaza

in a membrane of liquid light. Like the gold (not adobe)
the Spaniards thought they saw, coffers as wide as sky
over Seven Cities. Lydia pulls on her coat, pushes on ribbon,
remembers there's jewelry to be sold, turquoise and silver
flashing like eye-lets along the streets of the plaza.
These days, under the shade of the portal, there's the blue

of lapis and sapphire, too. All the colors of sky
remind Lydia of dawn, on the mesa, digging. Ribbons
of pale blue embedded in rock and aching for silver.
Now the stone-cold cuff on her wrist jolts her back to the plaza,
the bracelets for show and sell, cupped in the pale blue
of a tourist's cashmere gloves. Not unlike adobe

cast into bricks and walls, hugging windows ribboned
in Virgin Mary ultramarine. Bells swing and ring the silver-
toned song of the cathedral. It's a late Mass, the nave a plaza
of bowed heads. Where Lydia prays, the vault is a blue
arc from mountain to mesa, over the endless adobean
earth. Lydia knows it as the one, limitless sky

that cradles everyone from above—the caricaturist, silver-
haired, at his booth, the Mexican girls skipping in the plaza,
the santero wrapping up Saint Agnes in crisp blue
tissue paper. It's October. The day feels old as adobe,
new as the drugstore's loopy neon sign (sky-
high and glowing), fluid as the clouds' unruly ribbons.

My hair is silver, thinks Lydia, *the veins in my hands are large
and blue; my legs are earth-bound adobe. The plaza floats
on time's swirling ribbons. I'm swaddled; I'm half-swallowed in sky.*

Sestina de Santa Fé

Otoño sopla hojas en el pelo de mujeres. En la plaza,
Lydia alimenta las palomas—plumas iridiscentes y azules
en el sol mandarina. Es la tarde y adobe,
aplasta los hoteles estilo-pueblo contra un cielo
que los aguanta y estabiliza. Su falda está herida de cintas,
cosida con chorreras—terciopelo, negro y plata.

Los fiesteros derriban las puertas de La Fonda, azules
rompevientos y sombreros de vaqueros. Girados del adobe,
ellos corren junto a Lydia como un tornado. Una mirada al cielo
los aturde, por un momento, y se hacen una cinta
de risas estridentes. La luz del sol desciende en plata,
viaja por los canales metálicos, envolviendo la plaza

en una membrana de luz líquida. Como el oro (no el adobe)
que los españoles creyeron ver, los cofres anchos como el cielo
sobre las Siete Ciudades. Lydia tira de su abrigo, empuja cintas,
recuerda que hay joyas que vender, turquesa y plata
que destellan como espejos en las calles de la plaza.
Estos días, bajo la sombra del portico, hay azul

de lapislázuli y zafiro, también. Todos los colores de cielo
hacer que Lydia se acuerde del alba, en la mesa, cavando. Las cintas
azul pálido empotradas en la piedra, llamando a la plata.
Ahora el brazalete frío en su muñeca la trae de subito a la plaza,
las pulseras para ver y vender, ahuecada en el azul
de los guantes cachemira de un turista. Similar al adobe

moldeado en ladrillos y paredes, abrazándose a las ventanas encintadas
en el ultramino de la Virgen Bendita. Las campanas de plata
de la catedral tañen y cantan. Es una Misa tardia, la nave una plaza
de cabezas inclinadas. Dónde Lydia ora, la bóveda es un arco azul
de montaña a mesa, sobre la tierra interminable de adobe.
Lydia sabe que éste es el unico, ilimitado cielo

que acuna a todos desde arriba—el caricaturists con pelo de plata
en su puesto, las chicas mexicanas que saltan en la plaza,
el santero que envuelve a Santo Agnes en papel azul
crujiente. Es octubre. El día se siente vieja como el adobe,
nuevo como el anuncio de neón rojo de la farmacia (cielo-
alto y resplandeciente), fluido como las nubes, revoltosas cintas.

Mi pelo es plata, piensa Lydia, *las venas en mis manos son grandes*
y azules; mis piernas son adobes de la tierra. Esta plaza flota
en las cintas del tiempo. Estoy envuelta; estoy medio-tragada en cielo.

Clouds

How we know them without seeing:

I am looking down, fingers tight at the weed root
and pulling. The sting of the June sun migrates,
shoulder to shoulder and then, as if laying down
their white palms, a chill starts, each bead of sweat
refrigerates; I tilt nearly to earth. And I dream

of that summer, of blonde best friend Elizabeth
from Massachusetts who stood at the window
of our little Santa Fe rental spouting *Os*, crooning
their multitudinous shapes: *battleship, woman
giving birth, wooly mammoth* marching across
the western sky. Or the shadow that crawls across

the book I read for hours then sleep to, then wake
in fear for the spider creeping over my hand.
But no, it's just the moving white I don't have to
turn to, relieved. Or I am standing in the kitchen

and evening descends in the middle of the day
like a whale-bird, like an unexpected eclipse,
till it moves on and the sun cocks its head
toward the world again. And I don't have to see,

and it is enough to watch them in the mind—
snow-white, mansion-like, cut out against the wide
New Mexico blue, tumbling over the Sangres

in the summer afternoons, in droves, like they have
for millions of years and will, sometimes swift,
sometimes with rain, sometimes just floating
pure pleasure into the sightless hearts of children.

Days Like This

Shoulder to shoulder, with our sun umbrellas
and stadium seats, baseball caps and tubes

of SPF 30, I see the cashier from the carnicería
on Cerrillos, the dot.com retiree, the roofer

from high on Agua Fria Rd., the high school
teacher and downtown jewelry-maker.

And their children—ponytails, midriffs,
Raiders T-shirts, high-top Keds. This is a city

of markets, fiestas, community days, 4th of July
pancake breakfasts. If familiarity can no longer

gather us, then fry bread and Navajo tacos—
no matter how long and slow the line—

or a tortilla and bowl of green chile stew.
Grandma sits next to me on the curb

with no more short term memory. She tells
Serafina, her fidgety great-grand-girl,

about the way her father used to keep butter cold
in 1926 on the porch of the house in Española.

A system of shelves and wet canvas in the shade,
chilled by the summer breeze. Fina says *Wow,*

Grandma, you ARE old, and swings her monkey
purse over her left shoulder. These days

the city seems split in isolated sections—
east-side, Airport Road, Park Plaza,

and Casa Solana. The eighty year old
next to me says, in his day, all Santa Feans

lived in all the neighborhoods, at fisticuffs
or pleased as sardines. Today, it's the saving

grace of the Pet Parade: goldfish bowls
in red wagons, a golden retriever in tails,

someone's ferret in disco glitter. Is it
dogs in drag that bring us together?

There's a pueblo song that calls
the four directions so many times

I nearly believe we have come here
for some kind of blessing. Like the bones

of the skeleton, in that Hispanic folktale,
coming together to grant the courageous

the chance to do good. Or the Puritan,
Jonathan Edwards, writing *persons of all*

nations and all conditions. These four
third-graders, dressed up like daisies

and tethered to three family cats, form
some kind of unlikely and fabulous family.

And here we are. My sister says, *stop*
asking me and just eat your chicken-wrap

burrito thing. When she leans forward
I see the purple shadow on her lower back—

mark of the Moors, the doctor told Mother,
distant remnant of old, bloody Spain.

There are no simple answers here, just
a chubby blonde girl throwing candy

from a wheelbarrow, the strangers
across the street rubbing upper arms,

the seams of the city zipping up
at the threshold of donkeys and pet snakes.

The old man says *a veces la gente necesita
frotar codos*. It's true, we'll never
own things equally, agree and agree,
but there are days like this, lucky crush

and mosaic of blue jeans, baby bags,
sun hats and cowboy boots. He's right,

of course. Unlikely, mismatched, contentious.
Sometimes, people just need to rub elbows.

New Mexico Fragments

1.

The sky's a triplet—
indigo, navy, dusty pink.
Thirteen gargantuan ravens.
Bits in their beaks; Asian eyes.
Cheeky moon playing Jupiter.
I count nineteen black branches
and Lorca's three gold letters:
SUN.

2.

The curve of the horizon
and white interior walls.
Which is to say,
a woman and a man
in a room of light,
and the earth supine
under a violet sky.
Is to say, the ceremony
of the body. A hand wanders
to a chip of wulfenite,
a mile away from the arrowhead,
dug up. To say,

I pull the clay up and out,
round and high as I am.

3.

We cannot explain our love of mountains,
clay-red, dotted with piñon, chamisa, yucca.
Perhaps it is the expanse between them,
the sky which fills the space, immense,
the breath opened up like a holy book
blank and ever-blue, on and on.

4.

Seeing O'Keeffe's "Patio Door"
we cannot but think of the tongue,
the tongue on fire. It floats,
as does the oblique darkness of door,
the adobe wall going left,
the sky's blue mist lifting.

Here is the eye's ruse, suspension,
the leaf gone green and hot yellow.
The breath. The utter silence.
Gone aloft.

5.

Nothing grows in this earth
without diligence and cut knuckles.
I nurse broccoli, eggplant,
invoke the Rio Grande,
capture a cup of rainwater
and mete it out meticulously
with cracked and unwashed hands.

6.

*Why have you come
and who follows you
and how many new houses
and another paved road
and I'm telling you
I love this place because
so many do not live
here and here and there,
and there.*

7.

At Malpais I thought the cold would break
my bones. Your charts were useless;
your eyes went blind with the sky's glut
of stars. You crushed the last glowing ember,
said *don't touch me* and *I can die now,
why wait for something less than this.*

8.

So much snow we telemark
from our front door. The dogs

wander clueless over white
and the neighbor girls pack jars

with snowballs, label them, line
the top of the back yard wall.

They read *F-E-B-2-0-0-6* and *X*
and Meghan says the last one's
for a miracle, so it never melts.

9.

What the high desert gives to your name:

one more wild chamisa,
the mesa striated with iron-red,
spider-web cracks on the windshield

and the monsoons, finally, one afternoon,
the smell of spruce and creosote
in their wake, all night, saying.

Follow Me

Who hasn't driven north, up and over La Bajada Hill in dark December, to see the lights of Santa Fe unfurled—colcha, snowflake, electric mosaic? Hasn't wandered the evening streets just to trace the silhouettes of walkways, houses and hotels, counting farolitos? Hasn't driven past the Christmas tree lot on Rodeo Road just to get a whiff of fir, pine and spruce through the dashboard heating ducts? Hasn't heard the downtown sound of cathedral bells muffled in snow wafting in wafers onto wrought iron and woolen elbows? Has not looked up from St. Michael's Drive to the Sangres to search for the snow-covered horse's head? And who hasn't found a kitchen off San Ildefonso Road just to get out of the cold, down a half-dozen *biscochitos,* or knead the dough for sufganyot? Hasn't sipped a free cup of homemade cocoa on Christmas Eve, a gift from residents who live along Canyon Road? Has not walked the ice-milked sidewalks of Water Street and found themselves flat on their back then pulled up by some stranger saying, "Whoa, you went down like a ton of adobe bricks!" And who hasn't left town for the heart-bending dances at Santo Domingo then driven back to mark the little pines on the I-25 median, tinseled by some group of anonymous daredevils? Has not seen a kiva fireplace adorned with advent calendar, Menorah, bear fetish *and* ceramic Santa Claus? Hasn't feasted on turkey with piñon and green chile stuffing, red chile mashed potatoes, tortillas on the side? And who hasn't followed their grandmother lugging a wooden crèche from house to house during *las posadas,* the holy family looking for a place to stay, setting it down on someone's porch then driving away? And the dry colds so cold you want to drench them, and the stars so close you want to lick them? He who hasn't; she who has not, they who never have but are looking for a place to stay on some bone-cold Santa Fe night—follow me; this is the place; this way is the way.

Hush

she said

to the man
next to her

mid-narrative

in the din

of ten thousand
chanting

burn him

as the fire dancer
finally

dips his torch

to the wide
white skirt hem

of Zozobra

open-mouthed
writhing

I want to feel this
all of us
once a year

speaking
with one voice

Part Two

And They Called It Horizon

I.

Today we say Santa Fe, our *Santa Fé*
in the *sierra madre*, in the cradle between
the Pecos Mountains, *Cerro Piñon*,
Tano Point, *Caja del Rio, Tetilla* Peak.

But there was a time, long ago,
before names, dream before dream.
Haleeh, principio, the beginning.

It was a seed, imagine it, smaller
than the eye's dark pupil, smaller
than the tiniest yellow idea of seed,
and tinier. Inside, the dream
of something blue and unbelievably wide,
something rising to blue, *algún encuentro
magnífico de marrón y azul.*

And the seed there, buried.

Perhaps it was the eye behind the eye
of some great Being, or the eye
of a fantastic explosion, or the spot
on the tail-flick of a lizard
with red and black ridges on his back.

The seed nestled inside what became an orb,
an orb hurtling through indigo space,
then a spinning, whirling mass of blue
become this planet we call Mother Earth.

And it hung there, at the center,
weaving a garment of brightness.

And the warp was the white light of morning;
and the weft was the red light of evening;
and the fringes were sky-water falling;
and the borders the dewy rainbows of afternoons.

Cielo-agua que cae,
arcos iris arqueando.

The seed, buried in the earth
we later called Pangaea,
Laurasia, Gondwanaland,
the earth's first continents.

And the sea floor moved and kept moving
under magnetic waves, tectonic shifts,
plates going up and over and under.
The land rising up, volcanic,
to the east and to the north,
and to the northwest and the southwest.

The seed, the Being's eye finally opening
its lid, or the explosion bursting forth,
or the black spot moving back and forth
on the tail of this earth. Here, in this place,

geh, geh, geh, geh,
warp, weft, sky-water,
than pi, thamu tsan,
arcos iris.

What came from the seed emerged
into some unbelievable expanse
of sky tempered only by mountains
above and right and left, then a blanket

of brown and green and gold
unfolding to the south.
The line of the horizon, the sky-vault
resting like an ocean in the cradle of this place.

Before time, before memory.

This is how it began, before we were born,
before anyone called anything *tierra,*
geh, madre, shigan, Santa Fe, home.

II.

Millipede, darkling beetle, picture-winged fly.

The stink bug finds its likeness
in the shadows of windblown *welchii,*
winterfat, bristlecone pine, bigleaf sage.

Psorothamus scoparius, erioganum
umbellatum, sulfur buckwheat.
This is their sound, a quarry of names.

And here the small thunder of creature-feet:
dwarf shrew, western pipistrelle,
mogollon vole, rock pocket mouse.

The Zuni prairie dog and family clan
abandon their burrow, climb up
into the spring sun, lean and hungry.

The feed and starve, feed and starve,
of the tassel-eared squirrel
and ponderosa pine,
their symbiotic hum.

Then a larger thunder: elk, mountain lion, coyote.
The wapiti's resounding call, antlers clacking
in the sunset wings-sound of pygmy nuthatch,
brown creeper, mountain chickadee, dark-eyed junco.

Eye-spot, explosion, the creatures of shadow and air.
Cellular, ancestral—bridging now and there.

III.

In the beginning the People lived in the darkness of underground. One day the Mole visited them. The People asked if there was another world beside the one they lived in. The Mole told them to follow him. The People formed a line behind the Mole as he began to dig his way up. Each took the soil he loosened and passed it back to the next, and to the next, to the back of the line. This is why the tunnel closed behind them and they could never go back. The Mole led them to a place of sunlight and blue sky. This is the end; this is the beginning of their story.

IV.

They stood, dizzy with light,
the blue an enormous bowl
inverted above them.
And there was a seam
that sewed up earth and sky,

and they called it horizon,
and they traced it
with pointed fingers,
turning in place,
all the way around.

After a while they sang
they moved their feet.

After a while their tongues,
their ribcages, their knees
and ankles and toes stilled
to the crawl of thunderclouds
and mountains song.

They slept.
And then, they got to work.

V.

Our way is nomadic, home
is the wind between us
and over our heads as we
move, settling the earth
lightly and brief.

VI.
Our way is rooted, we build
the kiva deep and round.
Our houses cluster, emerge
from earth in a crowd.
We keep water, keep mountain
close—chambers of the heart.

VII.

Our ways study the rise
and downward slope of water,

its breath, configuration
of seed and sprout,
the moodiness of trees,
the sky-murmurs between moons
become sounds on our tongues,
the tales we pass down.

The little ones make stories
of these, ditties less grand;
we find them laughing.

This is another way
we know ourselves.

VIII.

This place is benevolence, yes,
this place can destroy us.

To the north, to the south and west
they disappeared, leaving
their cliff dwellings, hand-holds
and toe-holds, vertical routes.

We know of days when the land
denied them; we know of days
when the water ran out.

The earth commands, demands
a meticulous reverence, or else.

IX.

The sea is distant; the small river
that runs through here, fed
by the red-dusk mountains,
empties into another one, greater,
going there. It took some time,
against the southward current,
mouth to mouth,
for the news to come.

What kind of creature
carries a man like this?

They say your ancestor—*Nihippus*—
began to the east of this place,
on the great plains, and then,
like the old ones, disappeared.
The horse returns in another form,
enormous, under white-faced men
who carry fire in their hands,
belly, breast.

X.

The cyclone leaves blood on the land—
hoof prints, imprints of heeled boots,
sounds twisting the tongue: *caballo,
tierra, oro, alma, villa de santa fé.*

XI.

We carry, burn, bury the dead.
Sometimes we must leave them
where they fell. Animals take them
into their mouths, cry out the sound
that forever haunts our dreams.

XII.

The maps dizzy us with shifting
boundaries. Cartographers burn
the night oil, labor into dawn,
and we are given new nation-names,
again. Their fingers ache as they draw
and smudge, erase, dry up pens.

Incalculable, what we want,
create, what we have lost.

XIII.

Trappers, traders, cavvy boys,
misfits and mountain men
make the journey on horse,
in caravans, on the rutted road
from Missouri to Santa Fe.

Where the trail ends the square
begins—auctions, food stands,
dry goods and games of chance.
The fuss of horses and burros
under heavy packs, men with maps,
their slaves and hangers-on.

XIV.

From dirt to rut to cobblestone
to asphalt, foot and hoof,
to wagon wheel and hot black rubber.

How many leather mocs and petticoats,
how many hats have blown
and been chased
along these streets?

How many fingers on this map?

XV.

The village, *villa*, city unfolds
from the Palace of the Governors
to adobe roofs stepping up and down
into neighborhoods climbing
the *Sangres*, spilling north,
west, south, keeping to runoff,
snow, river, the images of water
we harbor in the mind's eye,
remember.

XVI.

If we look into windows,
into doors and back yards,
if we listen, there is the hum
of many tongues. And on the streets,
the panoramic spectrum
of eyes and skin.

XVII.

Day laborer, legislator, teacher, grocer,
shop owner, custodian, historian, gardener,
and those who drive the buzz of the city
all day all night, its steady drone.

XVIII.

Silversmith, painter, dancer, poet,
santero, sculptor, novelist, potter
and those who tell
their twilight dreams,
the city's singing mouth.

XIX.

And they come: on foot, over the borders,
by train and by car. Their luggage creates
a drum-sound beating over sidewalk
seams; they open their coin purses,
their wallets, they check in.

XX.

She sits up, climbs out of bed.
On her way to the kitchen
she wakes them. The black and white
of her uniform streaks from stove
to table to sink. Husband and children
wander into the room, half-awake, sit.
School bags, lunch boxes, half-
pairs of shoes crowd the back door.

Three stops on the way to work—
day care, engine shop, school—
then to the downtown hotel
where she pulls into a parking space
dabs out the stain on her pant leg,
steps out.

XXI.

The tourist thanks the waitress
as she lays down the check, asks
Are you from here? "Yes."
For how long? "Forever,"

and the man looks confused,
half-nods, almost opens his mouth.

XXII.

How to say this: seed, sky-vault,
mountains, symbiotic hum.

The Mole who visited them.

Benevolent place,
place of destruction.

The land cradling us, the land
the colors of our many faces,
skin. And we say Santa Fe,

our *Santa Fé,*
in the sierra madre,
in the cradle between

the Pecos Mountains,
Cerro Piñon, Tano Point,
Caja del Rio, Tetilla Peak.

This place on the tongue,
on our hands, on the soles
of our feet, and sweeping
around us, tracing a circle

from here to here as we turn,
all the way round,

and we call it horizon,

and we call it *geh, madre,
shigan, tierra,* Santa Fe,

home.

Part Three

Childhood

Floating, I hear sounds unlike my own.

Coo of syllables, coo cradles.

La tierra roja que mueve abajo.

Avalanche of history, with blood.

A mother-house, father-house.

The five plus one, cacophonous.

Mis dedos chicos, siempre hábiles.

Intuition. Politeness denies it.

The man infamous, car dangerous.

I give him no voice, no face, no hands.

Marauder, plunder of marauders.

Adolescent of the wails become words.

Así, tinta en el página.

Secret books. The looping black marks.

Where the silence, silence was.

And now, this rocky noise.

Letters to Wherever You Are

We write *Dear Diego, Dear Catherine,*
Dear Grandfather, Sweet Sister-Dear,

as if paper and ink travel the air
between now and then, here
and wherever you are.

What we did not say, couldn't,
wished we'd said, now have to—

I want you to know, remember,
it's clear now, everything you said

flutters across the page.

We imagine a place, a moment,
when these appear in your hands
like strange birds, delicate,
weathered from the trip.

They open their small mouths.

Devotion lasts, and it is sung
in the voices of those of us
who are left behind,
making peace with the incomplete,
inarticulate, half-said.
The past is past and still
we write, fold, send, believe

they arrive in the place
between now and the day
their zig-zag flight mimics

the one we'll take
when we, too, disappear.

Once, a nestling fell
from the rafters of the porch
and lay like a missive
on our front step. Its feathers
spread to reveal the thinnest
layer of bird-skin, pulsing
with tiny veins. Too small

to fly, we put it back in the nest,
up high, with five siblings
who knocked it out again.

Once, it opened its mouth as if
to feed, and what came out
was half breath, half sound,
from some world that wished
to take it back and did, later
that day, when its shivering

stilled. We felt culpable.
We had touched it, sullied
the world it fell out of.

These letters feel safe, reach
out to you who we've loved
from this tenuous distance—

draw the flight line between us—
honor the fact that we are still
here with our earthy language

written, folded, sent to you
in ink, on paper, on the wind,

wing-like, into the nest of your palms.

Art and Tennis Shoes

*written with students at Monte
del Sol Charter School, 2008*

In Santa Fe there is art
and tennis shoes

comfortably worn.

No tripping, smacking,
or bombing.

Shoelaces, home.

There is foot-love,
God-love,
leather-words
and yellow
Mexican food.

At your feet,
one big
alpaca knot.

Home is
your totally cherry kitchen,
and a comfortable bed,

oven food,
dumpster-kitchen love.

Crazy parents on fire!

Family ties—
enchiladas,
dirt and green gum
on the sidewalk.

One adobe, sleeping.

Home is piñon
sycamore, smoke
up the chimney.

Nikes and anklets
all strung up!

The curtains open,
the yellow sun
shines in, vines
of bright light.

The smell of chile
and kielbasa,
blooming.

Mid High, 1976

Where Mayor Coss and Marge sit now, the present-day
city hall, was once the nurse's office, the principal's,
half a classroom, maybe a textbook storage room
in the old Mid-High. If I look hard, it reappears.

Like a half-way house between junior high and high school
most ninth graders in the city got a ride or bused there
for one year as the mercilessness of puberty waned
and adulthood began. At lunchtime, they let us out

onto the downtown streets and we'd walk down Lincoln
to the old Woolworth's for a fifty-cent Frito pie
then plant ourselves on the plaza and make lists
of every boy or girl we loved, who ignored us,
and just who said she was going to break up
with him after he pretended he didn't know her.

The year before they shut down Mid-High my father
taught ninth grade, and I went there. It was bad enough
to be the daughter of one of the strictest teachers. Worse,
we drove to school in his prized Chevy '56, a monstrous white
behemoth among sleek yellow Mustangs and Corvettes.
I imagined the eyes of everyone were on us as arrived,

so I took to pretending to tie my shoes on the approach,
then waited for the first bell to slink out. My father
didn't even comment. At 14 the world is one big eyeball
staring at and through as if to shrink you to pebble-size
so I used to finger the globe in history class, whisper
all the countries I'd slip into silently, a radio journalist,

a bodiless voice over the airwaves, safe. About mid-year
some glitch in the electrical system made the Chevy honk
when Dad turned right. Each morning we drove St. Francis
to Paseo de Peralta with an obligatory wide right turn
around the post office to our parking space. For three weeks,
we wailed our approach from 500 feet off and everyone

turned to laugh. Dad got out, apologized, and the crowd waited
till after the bell to see me finally lift my head, grab
the passenger door handle and slide out. Every day
was imminent death. Then, one Friday, a boy I worshipped,
who never noticed me, walked up to the car, shifted his books,
and said, *This car is bitchin', aren't you in my English class,*

*my mom has a broken-down Impala, that honking thing
I think my uncle can fix, don't be embarrassed,
someday you'll probably tell everyone about this.*

I Won't Pretend

I dream a hum creeping through flagstone
like silver nettles, their purplish trumpet-blooms,
their prickly stems catching skin. I had gone to war
with them in the back yard, watering and pulling,
watering and pulling, as if my life depended on
their nothingness, absolute. Like the summer

in Rhode Island when I cleared a path into woods,
three months of sawing, hauling, hacking my way
through moose maple, ivy, white birch, and post oak
to create a trail to what I called "Inspiration Rock."
My sense of accomplishment felt complete,
the neatness of the open path, my tenaciousness,

as if the woods were *meddlesome, in the way*.
Accomplishment, complete, just for a moment
until the dreams began, men with steel helmets
descending from wooden boats, wading the shallows
to shore and wanting a way through, a way through
that muck against every aching hollow of want—

riches, land, redemption, abandonment—

and no matter how often some say this is the way
of the world, I wake up to rare, summer rain,
see the nettles peeking through and imagine the hum
that sprouted them, the story they're telling,
and what my pulling will lead to, one thing, next,
and another. And I won't pretend, lie to you

that I won't keep yanking them out. Here I am,
how many generations down. Here
is my infinitesimal enlightenment.

History, Apology

Long ago, in a class with N. Scott Momaday,
after reading his *Way to Rainy Mountain*,

considering a blurb on the back cover that read:
"This book nags at the White man's conscience,"

a twenty-something woman declared
that she would not and could not feel guilty

for terrible things her ancestors had done
that she had no part of, and hated.

Michelle, a seventh generation New Mexican,
fingers tacos in a booth at Tomasita's, says

*It's hard to live this way—Hispanic, Latina—
whatever you want to call me, when I do love*

*our traditions, when mother's side claims pure
Spanish blood, and knowing Oñate*

*and the others tore through this land hell-bent
on conversion, ownership, blood on their hands.*

Was there no one like me, then, against these ways?
And Luis, on the La Luz Trail, showing me

hoary cress, wild candytuft, Alpine clover, saying
Which part of me is Navajo grandmother,

*Chicano father, White mother? Feet to femurs,
pelvis to pecs, shoulder blades to the top of my head?*

Sometimes, I don't know where each begins and ends;
they rage at each other in my veins. Someday,

I am going to write a letter to each man in me,
Indian, Mexican, White, who never forgets.

"Shé éí Valerie yinishyé—I know there is no way
to sever the blood ties that tether me to my ancestors,

to history. They are the umbilical that roots me
in the land. I grieve for what my Spanish ancestors

wrought as a result of ignorance, greed, want,
and the dictates of far-off governments.

And if they also brought forms of beauty
(here, on the streets of this capital city)

I remember that there are no adequate reparations.
No. I apologize. I realize my obligation to honor

the survivors and their ways as if, one snowy afternoon,
I come upon their cave dwelling, camp, village, pueblo,

a half-woman asking for food, hearth, finished limbs,
and a heart made complete by association."

She Has Come to Us
after the Apache

The moon's horse is a black mare;
her nose, the place above her nose,
is white mist. Her ears, of the small
lightning bolts, are moving back and forth.
Her tail, too, is pale froth. She has come
to us. The moon's horse is a black mare—
orange-black, red-black, indigo-black.
The moon's horse has come out to us.

Part Four

Easter Pilgrims

for Andrea Martínez
1959–2008

The old one, buttoned up, wind hard at his back.
The old one, pushed forward on his staff.

I wake up

>from some fog, bent sun,
hypnotic drone of the car engine

to the Easter pilgrims, everywhere, on the shoulder.
Still a week out, on foot, a hundred miles
from the Santuario de Chimayo.

Because you are gone, my sister, the pilgrimage—

>this one, each spring,
the Haj, even the pagan
cure-for-cancer pledge run

unlocks it:

What is my church, Old Man with a Staff?
How do you know yours? Believe?

Because I cannot, six months after your death,
feel you near me, I want to join the severest ones,
on their bloody knees.

Theirs is a certainty, yes, and I have gone the other way.

The rain starts, here, on the interstate.

The man, now far behind, is pelted with raindrops,

       triangular,
       arrow-like,
       honed by wind.

He walks on.

I do not know where you are, for sure, though I am given
certain definite options by those who do:

       heaven
       reincarnation
       absolutely nothing.

I have chosen, instead, the hush and no
of unknowingness
and the images I give it—

       black hole, mountain
       fog, river mud—

things we cannot see through.

Your way, Old Man, sings of some old
certainty, deep in the belly.
I remember it, recognize it again
from our childhood days, Sweet Sister.

It is sharp, sacrificial, the vertiginous certitude
of these teenagers, old couples, men
with their spare boots slung over their backs.

They are dizzying, yes. Their beauty,
this clarity—it slays me.

El mundo al mundo
un sueño

Descubro el Buda en el traspatio,
 pintura negra en la madera,
la cabeza inclinó, la sonrisa tan tranquilo.
 Entonces el muerto viene
sobre el césped, las piedras del jardín,
 una cama de flores, sin el sonido,
las bocas silenciosas como bajo-la-tierra.
 No necesitamos cualquieras palabras,
el muerto y yo. Solamente imágenes,
 el mensaje que *ellos vienen*,
el pasaje secreto bajo la pared,
 la criaturas que suben,
el cielo sobre las nubes sobre el aire sobre la tierra,
 mundo al mundo, esta tarde,
alguien yo soy, alguien yo supe,
 las capas debajo las capas.

On the Road to Mictlán

> *After death, the Nahua people undertake a journey of nine obstacles on the way to a final resting place.*

On the family altar, just after her last breath,
they put down sugar skulls and sweet bread,
water and candles and incense,
the journey's sustenance—

        and so she goes

first to *Itzcuintlan*, the great river, tethered
to a tan-colored dog paddling furiously,
the numb soul dragged behind, all
worry, regret, memory—

        and if they have the strength

there is *Tepictli Monanamictlan*
where the dog disappears, and the soul
must find the keyhole between crashing mountains,
make herself quick and small and humble—

        and if she slides through

it's the *Hill of Flint Knives—Itzepetl—*
a billion wicked tips asking fearlessness,
the acrobatic flip from shank to shank, un-slit—

        and if she's unscathed

there is *Itzelcayan, Place of the Icy Wind*, whipping
the skin free. Only the *petate*, palm mat
placed by a devoted sister, in front of the altar,
can swaddle the soul free—

        and if she weathers this

it is *Panielcultac,* where the skin begins to fall
in folds and wrinkles. *Place Where the Bodies
Float Like Flags*, and matter moves to flying spirit—

                  and if she starts to disappear

there is *Timiminoloyan* of the Piercing Arrows,
rending the last bits of sinew and flesh,
unveiling the delicate heart—

                  and if she surrenders

it is *Teocoyolcualloyo* with its gnashing teeth,
where the heart is devoured and spit out
by the gods, a sky-blanket of diamonds, blood-red—

                  and if she paints between the stars

she becomes the Place of the Fog, *Yzmictlan Apochcaloca,*
where the blanket of the true soul
becomes the smoke of copal

                  and if she seeps from sun to sun

she comes to the place of the Nine Waters—*Chiconouhhapa*—

        ocean, river, melting snow,
        human tears, saliva, wet-desire,
        rain, god-slobber, dripping soul—

                  and if she bathes here

she arrives at the Navel of the World, *Chicunamictlán,*
where the little dog reappears, shows her
how to circle and paw and curl up perfectly—

                  sky, wet smoke, universe-flesh—

to rest and rest.

Trying to Understand

Now the gang members appropriate
the image of the Virgin Mary
of Guadalupe,

needled into skin,
screened onto cotton,
sprayed onto concrete
with boxy, leaning
gang tags, for protection.

The pallbearers wear her resplendent
on their T-shirts, one after another,
until she blurs under the casket,
the teenager with a bullet in his neck.

They feel him passing over.
They invoke her because pain
is the passing, the reaching through.

She knew it.
They know it.

They know it and know it.

Street Secrets

I thought I knew these city streets like the mole on my hip,
    knee scar, faint birthmark, but Molly takes us left

on Camino del Campo, right on West San Francisco,
    left on Park to Catron, Griffin, West Marcy,

past city housing, chain-link fencing, between adobe
    houses and newly stuccoed offices, one fat cat

on a crumbling porch step, and though I've driven every
    single Santa Fe street in my life, I don't know

this way downtown. Or the day I first bicycle across Cerrillos
    onto Monterey, Santa Cruz, East Street, Jay

and Quapaw, get lost on Navajo, Nambé and Cochiti
    —where's the bike route?—but I don't care

because there's *Que Suave*, the old Johnny's Market,
    snapdragons against an old wooden door

and Tibetan prayer flags strung between vigas. I hear
    conversations in French from one yard, Japanese—

is it?—from another, and Mariachis play "Las mañanitas,
    to great applause, from somewhere else.

Or it's late summer and I drive Miriam and Brenda south
    on Jaguar to see the new houses on Apache Knoll,

Valentine Way, Paseo del Sol, Solecito Loop. Someone is
    roasting green chile, maybe a whole burlap sack,

and I trace the rising and cascading rooftops while these two
    teenagers sing me everything text-messaged

to their little red and green framed screens, boys with crushes
    and words, and you think you know someplace,

you think you've traveled its city skin, but love isn't
    the familiar birthmark, the scar you trace

on your loved one's sunburned back. No, there's a new bruise,
    the end-of-summer freckles you delineate, surprises

that keep us taking one sudden right or left turn in town, even
    if it stops with a dead end, because loving a place

means taking it in our hands, again, tracing the same lines
    with senses turned on, knocked out of our workaday

dream, a wide-eyed old resident-turned-explorer, wandering
    the body of our beloved, ever-changing, old city.

Thistle Forest
for Paul

Whip lines on my lower legs
make a fine mesh in flesh,
and thistle-spines stick deep.

Red radiating. Threatening blood.

Walking into them—pale leaves
rise triangular and spine-tipped,
cradle a thunder of purple heads.

A sea of ghost-gray. Lavender horizon.

Post fire, on the Dome Wilderness Trail,
tree trunks lay like pick-up sticks.
Some stand like the fire-dead, dizzy
and charred, above a thistle-down sea.

From behind, you watch my calves
navigate jagged rocks, fallen tree trunks,
thistle after thistle.

A wicked mesh. I never flinch.

They are beautiful, rise up in the wake
of flames, acres of black.

You take my hand. No more waiting,
you love me: legs, whip lines,

a gray and lavender sea.

River Ode

Río de las Palmas
Rio Turbio
Guadalquivir
Río del Norte
Río Bravo
Río Grande

and the first
unintelligible names,
music in other tongues,

river, river, river, river

springing forth
from a murmuring earth.

You unfold
    over stick and rock,
        silt shifting,
            past moss,
                worm and mosquito,
                    cross footpath
                and dirt path,
            over the translucent feet
              of children, through
                  village, backyard,
                      under sun, orange-moon,
                        under wing:
                    butterfly, firefly, dragonfly
                      shimmering.
                  Lapping the tongues
            of cow, horse, bear, coyote,
        through gills,
      over scales and open eyes,
    under foot, under log

and board and bridge,
                under gaze, under canoe,
                                under swollen yellow plastic,
                between shoots and sprigs,
                through meadows,
deserts, dams, Falcon, Amistad, Anzalduas,
        into reservoirs
                and man-made lakes,
                        through cities,
                                by maquiladoras,
                                        migrant workers,
                        remnants of vineyards,
                                wheat fields and burial grounds,
                                        now gathering,
                now swelling, now rushing relentless,
overflowing, making things list—trailer home, phone booth,
swing set—pulling down corn stalks and stop signs, cottonwoods,
        tearing everything from their sinewy roots,
                then slowing,
                        dwindling,
                                vanishing,
                        into the white hot,
                                and
        trickling
                        and
                                threading
                winding its way
                        toward the presence of,
                                near the presence of,
                                in the presence of
                                noise of waves,
                                sheen of sand,
                                murmuring,
                                and into
                                the Gulf,

                                río, río, río

                                        gone.

From beyond the dewy expanse of space
the earth is revealed as clouds
whirling over water,
everywhere,
and seven bodies of land
with their spidery veins.

Amazon-Ucayali. Yangtze.
Congo. Zambezi. Orinoco.
Ganges. Mississippi. Volga.
Euphrates. Ob-Irtysh

where the land gives way
to movement, water
sculpting a body
into curves,
depressions,
hills and mountains.

And the song the rivers give
to the soil, mute in itself,
music when it loosens
and joins the water,
mid-symphony,

the sound of stream
and earth's creatures
waking.

And so you are memory,
canyon with its ribbon-strata,
water at the bottom,
intricate map of history,
geological; ancestry,
creature-shell
embedded in rock.

Skulls and bones.
Primitive tools.

Here is the Mayan virgin plummeting
into the sacred cenote, water-fed,
river-blue. Almost lifeless, watch her
float to the surface, eyes cast over,
spurting messages from the dead.

River-Monger:
we siphon you to cities
so the beds go dry.
We litter you with plastic,
so the creatures gag.
We dump chemicals into you,
so the water thickens,
so the water darkens
and darkens,
and we drink you,
River-Dark,

our bones lies embedded in the strata.

You unveil us, River.
We are forgetful.

What we remember of our dreams
on the banks of our beds:
the hurricane's wild eye,
the ocean's steady-blue,
the near drowning,
the house dripping,
the under-the-back-door's seeping,
the buoyance, merciful,
water on the parched tongue,
river-blood, placental.

And more dreams
and more water
and consciousness unfolding
(gasping on the sand)
from sleep to human life
waking.

River-Ever:
the sun taking
the rain giving
the mountains melting
the oceans calling
emptying filling
breaking your banks
swallowing huts and mansions alike,
buoying the dreaming bodies of earth.

And the crops expanding
and expanding, river-milk
forever in our mouths.

River-Torrent
River-Nourisher

Nile, Huang, Paraná,
Tigris, Danube, Missouri,
Madeira, Río de la Plata,
Río Grande

waking
moving
witnessing

River Now Told,

telling and telling.

Home

Once we claim it for ourselves, we've lost it forever.
A mystery we cannot own—where space begins.

Behind the coyote fence, adobe wall, blue windowpanes
is someone I do not know who calls this place home.

We tug at blue, at mountains, at easements.
We put our names on the ground, and sing.

It slips out of our hands.

You say it isn't ground but sky.
Unrolled to the skirt-hem of the horizon.

You say land is secondary to air.
As if we bed down, as if we float there.

Home is a parcel of sunlight
or moon-cooled air. Imagine:

everyone up off the ground, hovering.
Not this world, I'm afraid. Another one.

Not place, but people. I settle where you are,
where they have been, where you want to go.

It is the feeling of proximity, a nearness
in space. Locks of hair and fingernails

are intermediaries, interlocutors,
wooly hearth till the loved ones get home.

She says we carry it around inside, no matter.
Santa Fe, Chicago, Tucson, Swaziland.

He says: *If only there were a way to make
the Sangres intestinal.* She laughs.

Cellular, perhaps. Deep in the bone marrow,
muscles, DNA. Home is consanguineous,

tethering body to body, from here
to contention, every new creation story.

Blast of atoms, Eve's sudden appearance,
behind the mole who emerged from earth.

From *Father* up there to *Mother*
to *Matter*, down here. The spiral helix,

down from heaven, or climbing up,
root-like, from the center of the earth.

Tierra o muerte. Yes,
there are places worth
fighting for, if only
we could claim them,
definitively, forever until now.

As if nothing changed,
as if there was a single
defining document,
as if there is nothing
to be shared, and no one
was descended from us,
or wishes for something else.

To put my name
on this square foot
demands so much.

When,
in my last hours,
when I forget
your face
and theirs
and everything
else, just lay me
down, here,
in her brown
and wrinkly
palms.

About the Author and the Artist

Valerie Martínez is a poet, teacher, translator, editor, and collaborative artist. Her books include *Absence, Luminescent, World to World, Each and Her, A Flock of Scarlet Doves: Selected Translations of Uruguay's Delmira Agustini*, and *Reinventing the Enemy's Language: Contemporary Writing by Native Women of North America*. The title poem of this book also appears in a limited, hand-press edition, *This is How It Began*, created by the Palace of the Governors Press. Valerie is a member of the core artist team of Littleglobe, Inc. which collaborates with diverse, intergenerational communities on large-scale collaborative works of art and performance. Valerie has taught at the University of Arizona, New Mexico Highlands University, Ursinus College, College of Santa Fe, Institute for American Indian Arts, University of New Mexico, and in the rural schools of Swaziland. She has a B.A. from Vassar and an M.F.A. from The University of Arizona. She was the Poet Laureate for the City of Santa Fe for 2008–2010.

Linda Swanson is chair of the Art Department at Santa Fe University of Art and Design. Her paintings and drawings have been shown nationally and are in the permanent collections of The Newark Museum and The Brooklyn Museum. The drawings in this book are part of a larger work, *Enough*, which consists of 340 drawings of snapshots from her family photo archive. In recording what is experienced, *Enough* retrieves and rearranges narratives and recognizes both the flow of everyday events and the marking of occasion. Linda lives in Santa Fe and Los Angeles with her husband and daughter.

Notes *and* Translations

"Blue Winding, Blue Way"

    mi linda…¿donde está tu mama / "pretty one…where is your mom?"

    p'oe tsawa, Tewa / "blue water"

"Days Like This"

    a veces la gente necesita frotar codos / "sometimes people just need to rub elbows."

"Follow Me"

    colcha / an embroidered bedspread or bed-cover, one of New Mexico's traditional Hispanic tapestries.

    pastelito, / a traditional Hispanic pastry, usually made for the holidays, two layers of pastry with a fruit and raisin filling in between, sugar-dusted and oven-baked.

    sufganyot / Hanukkah donuts

    las posadas / a nine-day celebration with origins in Spain, beginning December 16 and ending December 24. It is a yearly tradition for many Catholics and symbolizes the search by Mary and Joseph for a place where Jesus could be born.

"Hush"

    Zozobra / ("Old Man Gloom") is the name of a giant marionette which is built and burned every autumn to open the Fiesta de Santa Fe, releasing the city and its people from the sadness, bad luck and evil spirits of the preceding year.

"And They Called It Horizon"

>*Haleeh* / Diné/Navajo for "it comes into existence"
>
>*geh* / Tewa word for "place," sometimes spelled "que"
>
>*principio* / "beginning"
>
>*algún encuentro/magnífico de marrón y azul* / "some magnificent encounter/with brown and blue"
>
>*Cielo-agua que cae,/arcos iris arqueand* / "sky-water that falls/rainbow arching"
>
>*than pi, thamu tsan* / Tewa for "sunrise, daybreak"
>
>*tierra…madre* / "earth…mother"
>
>*shigan* / Diné/Navajo for "my home"
>
>*psorothamus scoparius, erioganum* / Latin names for broom dalia and sulfur buckwheat, native plants of northern New Mexico
>
>*caballo,/tierra, oro, alma, villa de santa fé* / "horse,/earth, gold, soul, city of the holy faith"

"Childhood"

>*La tierra roja que mueve abajo* / "The red earth that moves beneath."
>
>*Mis dedos chicos, siempre hábiles* / "My small fingers, always deft."
>
>*Así, tinta en el página* / "This way, ink on the page."

"History, Apology"

>*Oñate,* Don Juan de (1550 – 1624) was the conquistador generally attributed with establishing the first Spanish colony in the area of present-day Santa Fe. It eventually became one of Spain's most important

northern outposts. In return, the King of Spain named Oñate governor and *adelantado (governor)* of New Mexico. Oñate and his men faced the fierce opposition and resistance of the native peoples of North America. The Ácoma Pueblo rose in a courageous but ultimately unsuccessful revolt in 1692. Oñate severely punished the people of Acoma. Men over twenty-five had one foot cut off and were sentenced to twenty years of personal servitude to the Spanish colonists; young men between the ages of twelve and twenty-five received twenty years of personal servitude; young women over twelve years of age were given twenty years of servitude; sixty young girls were sent to Mexico city to serve in the convents there, never to see their homeland again, and two Hopi men caught at the Acoma battle had their right hand cut off and were set free to spread the news of Spanish retribution. Despite Oñate's best efforts, the colony did not quickly prosper, and the people blamed the governor for all their troubles. In 1607 Oñate, noting that he had already spent 400,000 pesos on New Mexico, asked to be relieved of the governorship. He returned to Mexico about 1609 to answer charges of maladministration. He was convicted of disobedience and mistreatment of the Indians and colonists. Oñate appealed the verdict and may have been successful in obtaining a pardon before his death.

"Easter Pilgrims"

Santuario de Chimayó. Built in the 1810's on sacred earth and famous for its miraculous healing powers, this small church is one of the most visited holy sites in New Mexico. It is located 24 miles northeast of Santa Fe. Each year, during Holy Week, thousands of people make the pilgrimage to Chimayó to visit the Santuario (sanctuary) and take away a bit of the churches sacred healing dirt. Pilgrims journey sometimes a hundred miles or more.

"World to World" (translation)
a dream

    I discover the Buddha in the back yard,
        black paint on wood, head tilted,
    smile so tranquil. Then the dead come
        over the grass, the garden stones,
    a bed of wildflowers, without sound,

    mouths silent as underearth.
We needn't have any words,
    the dead and I, just holy imagery,
the message they come, the secret
    passage under the wall, the creature
who climbs through, the sky
    over the clouds over the air over the earth,
world to world, this afternoon,
    someone I am someone I knew,
the layers beneath the layers.

"On the Road to Mictlán"

In Aztec mythology, Mictlán was the ninth level of the underworld, located far to the north. Except for warriors who died in battle, people who died when hit by lightning, and women who died in childbirth, people journeyed to Mictlán after death. The trip was difficult and took four years, but the dead were aided by the psychopomp, a leader and guider of souls.

www.ingramcontent.com/pod-product-compliance
Lightning Source LLC
Chambersburg PA
CBHW021015090426
42738CB00007B/793